500 CHAT GPT PROMPTS FOR EDUCATORS TOWARDS EXCELLENCE AND EASE OF TEACHING

DR DHEERAJ MEHROTRA

Contents

PREFACE

Technology enhances teaching effectiveness, engagement, and efficiency in today's fast-paced educational landscape. With the emergence of AI-driven tools like ChatGPT, educators now have a powerful resource to simplify lesson planning, personalize learning, and foster interactive classrooms. **500 ChatGPT Prompts for Educators Towards Excellence & Ease of Teaching** *is designed to be a practical guide for teachers, school leaders, and educationists who seek to integrate AI into their daily teaching practices. This book offers a comprehensive collection of prompts that can assist in lesson planning, classroom management, student engagement, assessments, professional development, and more.*

Each prompt is crafted to help educators maximize their efficiency, reduce workload, and enhance creativity in lesson delivery. Whether you want to design interactive quizzes, simplify complex concepts, or generate insightful discussion topics, this book is your AI-powered companion. Education is evolving, and so should our teaching methods. This book is not just about using AI; it's about transforming how we teach—making education more accessible, efficient, and innovative for the next generation of learners.

Let's embrace AI as a tool for excellence and redefine the future of education—one prompt at a time!

Dr. Dheeraj Mehrotra

I

500 Chat GPT Prompts for Educators Towards Excellence & Ease of Teaching

BONUS PROMPTS

For Educators & Trainers

"Explain [concept] to a 10-year-old with examples."

"Create a 45-minute lesson plan on [topic] including objectives, activities, and assessment."

"Summarise this chapter in simple points for classroom discussion."

"Design 10 quiz questions (MCQs) with answers for [subject/topic]."

"Prepare a short speech on [theme] for school assembly (3 minutes)."

For Students & Learners

"Explain the difference between [term1] and [term2] with examples."

"Generate study notes for my exam on [subject]."

"Write a 200-word essay on [topic]."

"Give 5 sample interview questions for [career/field]."

"Help me understand [concept] through a real-world example."

For Professionals & Office Use

"Write a professional email to [recipient] about [situation]."

"Summarize this document in bullet points."

"Create a project proposal outline for [initiative]."

"Generate a meeting agenda for our weekly review."
"Suggest a LinkedIn post about [achievement/event]."

For Creativity & Writing

"Write a short motivational story about [theme]."
"Give me 10 creative ideas for a classroom activity on [topic]."
"Write a dialogue between two characters discussing [issue]."
"Rewrite this paragraph in a more engaging way."
"Suggest 5 catchy titles for my article/book on [subject]."

For AI & Self-Improvement

"List 10 ways I can use ChatGPT effectively for my daily work."
"Give a step-by-step guide to learn [skill/subject] in 30 days."
"Create a daily schedule for balancing study, work, and fitness."
"Explain how AI can improve teaching and learning."
"Suggest 10 habits to increase productivity and happiness."

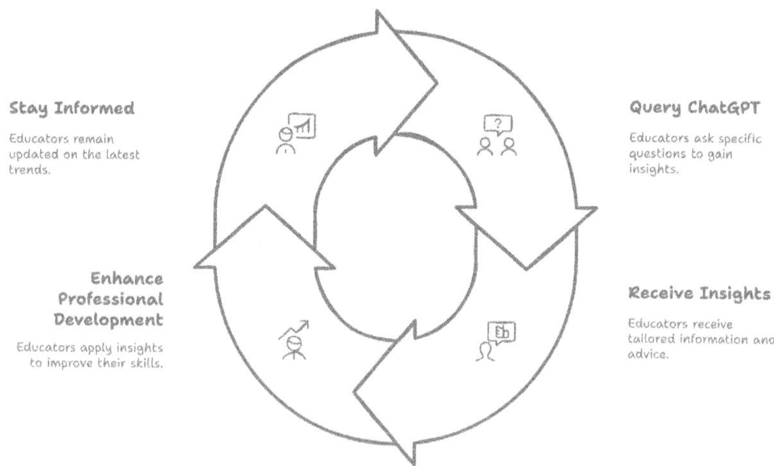

1. Please suggest a lesson plan for teaching [subject] to [grade level].

2. For [topic], develop a one-week unit plan that concentrates on [particular skill/concept].

3. Conceive of engaging activities that can be used to educate [subject] to [age group].

4. Please provide a step-by-step guide to educate [topic] in a way that is both enjoyable and participatory.

5. Suggestions for differentiating instruction for [subject] to accommodate a wide range of students are welcome.

6. Create a learning activity based on a project for [topic] centred around [theme].

7. Create an instructional plan that incorporates the use of technology in the teaching of [subject].

8. To educate [subject], recommend linkages that span many disciplines.

9. For a unit on [subject/topic], please include a list of essential questions.

10. You should create a grading rubric to evaluate student projects on [subject].

11. To correctly manage a noisy classroom, please provide some strategies.

12. A positive classroom culture can be built with the help of the following strategies.

13. What are some ways that I can manage disruptive behaviour in the classroom without making the problem much worse?

14. *Suggest activities to break the ice on the first school day.*

15. *It would be helpful if you could provide a checklist for organising the classroom.*

16. *How can I motivate kids to cooperate with classroom rules?*

17. *Make some suggestions about how to address disagreements between pupils.*

18. *During the lessons, provide solutions for managing time.*

19. *How can I make my classroom environment more welcoming to all students?*

20. *Encourage students to behave favourably by suggesting rewards and incentives.*

21. *To introduce [subject] to kids, create creative examples.*

22. *You should suggest using interactive games when teaching [subject/concept].*

23. *What are some ways that I can make [their topic] more relatable to them?*

24. *If you are teaching about [subject], please include some ideas for hands-on activities.*

25. *Make suggestions on how storytelling might be included in the classroom.*

26. *To what extent can I teach [subject] using examples from the real world?*

27. *Create questions for the class to discuss and debate on [subject].*

28. *To keep students interested in [the topic], please suggest strategies to employ multimedia.*

29. *Please suggest activities that could be done in groups on [the topic].*

30. *I have shy pupils; how can I make the lessons more interactive?*

31. *Make a test with ten questions with multiple choice answers on [the subject].*

32. *Please provide suggestions for formative assessment methods for [topic].*

33. Describe some examples of constructive criticism that can be applied to student essays.

34. Develop a checklist for pupils to use in their self-evaluation on [subject].

35. How can I make the most of the peer assessment process in the classroom?

36. Suggest evaluating the students' comprehension without using assessments.

37. Please provide some suggestions for questions that could be included on the exit ticket for [topic].

38. Construct a grading rubric for the presentations given by groups.

39. Is it possible to monitor the progress of students over time?

40. To motivate pupils, please suggest several ways to deliver feedback.

41. Please suggest educational apps that can be used to educate [topic].

42. What are some ways that I can improve my learning with Google Classroom?

43. Suggest how virtual reality could be used in [the subject] classes.

44. Suggest how [grade level] might be taught to code.

45. How can I make video lessons that are interesting and engaging for [topic]?

46. To use interactive whiteboards efficiently, please provide some tips.

47. Please suggest methods for incorporating artificial intelligence capabilities into the classroom.

48. For educational reasons, what are some ways that I can use social media?

49. Think of ideas for projects that can be done in collaboration online.

50. Make suggestions for how students might be taught about digital citizenship.

Streamlining Teacher Administrative Tasks

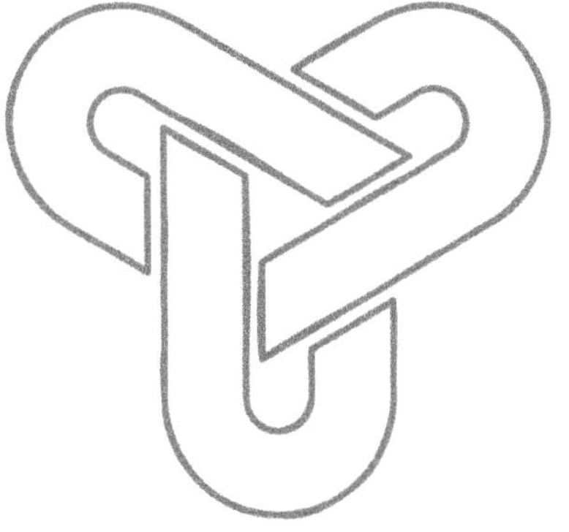

51. Development of Professional Skills

52. Suggest books or other materials that could help improve teaching abilities.

53. As a teacher, please advise on maintaining a healthy work-life balance.

54. How might I keep abreast of recent educational developments?

55. Give some suggestions on how to collaborate with your coworkers effectively.

56. Make suggestions for attending educational conferences and giving presentations at those conferences.

57. How can I make my teaching more effective with reflective practice?

58. Please recommend online courses for professional growth in [topic].

59. What are some ways that I might incorporate teaching mindfulness into my daily routine?

60. *You should compose a welcome letter to the parents at the beginning of the school year.*

61. *Describe some strategies that can be used to make parent-teacher conferences more productive.*

62. *Suggest how parents might be informed about their children's progress.*

63. *What are some ways that I can interact with parents in the classroom?*

64. *Create an email to parents informing them of an upcoming event at the school.*

65. *Methods should be provided to meet the worries of parents.*

66. Please suggest getting parents involved in their children's homework.

67. What are some ways that I can communicate with my parents using technology?

68. Please provide suggestions for evenings of family engagement.

69. Please provide suggestions on how to manage challenging conversations with parents.

70. Provide some suggestions for teaching students with attention-deficit/hyperactivity disorder (ADHD).

71. How may I modify lessons to accommodate students with difficulties learning?

72. *Kindly provide ways to create an inclusive classroom climate.*

73. *Help students with autism by providing them with educational resources.*

74. *In what ways may I make use of assistive technology in the classroom?*

75. *Offer suggestions for differentiating the teaching approach for gifted pupils.*

76. *Make available various instructional methods for students who have dyslexia.*

77. *Where can I find support for pupils struggling with emotional and behavioural issues?*

78. *Make suggestions for methods to work together with the staff of special education.*

79. *About [subject], please suggest art projects.*

80. *Assist in developing scientific experiments suitable for [grade level].*

81. *Produce a list of creative writing ideas appropriate for [age group].*

82. *Ideas for using games to teach mathematics are welcome.*

83. *Give some suggestions for educational activities that can be done outside.*

84. *Propose activities that involve drama to teach [subject].*

85. *Come up with entertaining trivia questions on [topic].*

86. *Suggest ways to celebrate the diversity of cultures in the classroom.*

87. *Make suggestions for how music might be incorporated into the lessons.*

88. *Please provide some suggestions to celebrate the school year's conclusion.*

89. *Please suggest techniques to increase student confidence in [topic].*

90. *Help pupils learn how to deal with stress by providing strategies.*

91. The question is, how can I inspire kids to have a growth mindset?

92. Please provide ways to motivate kids who are not performing well.

93. To teach pupils about mindfulness, please provide some ideas.

94. How can I assist students in establishing and achieving their academic goals?

95. Offer suggestions for methods to honour the accomplishments of students.

96. What are some practices that can be used to help pupils become more resilient?

97. What steps can I take to enable students to express themselves freely in a secure environment?

98. Suggest how students might be educated about the importance of mental health?

99. A lesson plan for teaching fractions to fourth graders would be appreciated.

100. Construct a lesson plan for the fifth graders to teach them about the water cycle.

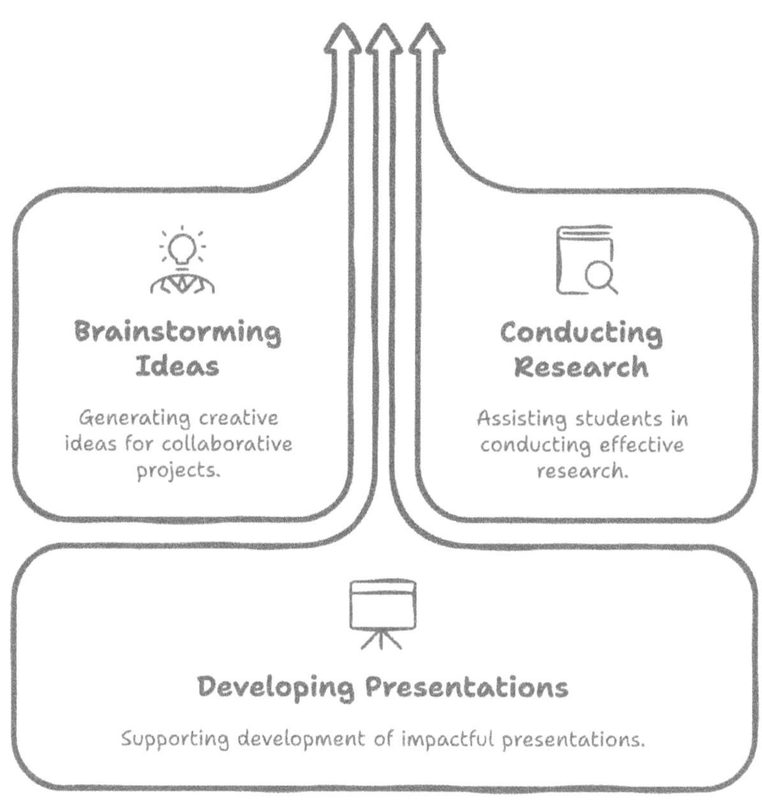

101. Students in middle school should be provided with activities that teach them about the solar system.

102. Make a detailed and step-by-step plan for teaching high school pupils how to write an essay.

103. Give some suggestions on how phonics can be taught to kindergarten kids.

104. To teach about the American Revolution, you should create a lesson plan.

105. To learn about environmental science, you should develop a project-based learning activity.

106. Give some suggestions on how art might be included in a historical lesson.

107. Please provide a list of questions about ecosystems necessary for a unit.

108. A grading criteria should be developed to evaluate the student presentations on climate change.

109. Make suggestions about how elementary school pupils can be taught to code.

110. Make a lesson plan for teaching Macbeth, a play by William Shakespeare.

111. The third graders should be provided with activities that teach them multiplication tables.

112. Make suggestions for how the scientific method might be taught through experiments.

113. To teach the fundamentals of geometry, you should develop a lesson plan.

114. *Educate students about the Civil Rights Movement by providing these suggestions.*

115. *Make suggestions for games that could be used to teach grammar.*

116. *You should develop a unit plan to educate the human body's systems.*

117. *Offer activities that teach students in the second grade how to read maps.*

118. *Please suggest other ways that high school students might learn about poetry analysis.*

119. *The periodic table should be taught using a lesson plan that you create.*

120. *To teach middle school students about financial literacy, please provide some ideas.*

121. *Give some suggestions on how elementary school kids might learn to tell stories.*

122. *Develop a lesson plan for teaching the fundamentals of coding to your students.*

123. *Activities should be provided to teach students about the life cycle of a butterfly.*

124. *Please suggest other ways that first graders can be taught about time.*

125. *Develop a lesson plan for teaching students about the factors that led to World War I.*

126. *Please provide some ideas for teaching the water cycle through hands-on activities.*

127. *Make some suggestions on how the idea of probability may be taught.*

128. *Develop a lesson plan for explaining ancient civilisations to your students.*

129. *Activities should be provided to teach the notion of gravity.*

130. *Please provide suggestions for teaching the writing process to students in middle school.*

131. *To teach the fundamentals of mathematics, you should develop a lesson plan.*

132. *Make suggestions for how the idea of photosynthesis might be taught to students.*

133. *Please provide suggestions for how the concept of fractions might be taught using examples from real life.*

134. *Develop a lesson plan for teaching the fundamentals of economics to your students.*

135. *To explain the notion of symmetry, you need to provide activities.*

136. *Explain the notion of time zones in a variety of different ways.*

137. *To teach the fundamentals of chemistry, you should develop a lesson plan.*

138. *Suggest how the concepts of force and motion can be taught to students.*

139. *Suggest how the concepts of area and perimeter can be taught.*

140. *Make a lesson plan for teaching the fundamentals of astronomy to your students.*

141. *Activities should be provided to teach the notion of volume.*

142. *What other ways might the concept of ratios and proportions be taught?*

143. *To teach the fundamentals of physics, you should develop a lesson plan.*

144. To teach the notion of probability through games, please provide some ideas.

145. Explain the notion of decimals in a variety of different ways.

146. Develop a lesson plan for teaching the fundamentals of biology to your students.

147. Activities should be provided to explain the notion of angles.

148. Make some suggestions on how the concept of percentages can be taught.

149. Provide suggestions for how to deal with a disruptive student.

150. Offer some suggestions for fostering a constructive atmosphere in the classroom.

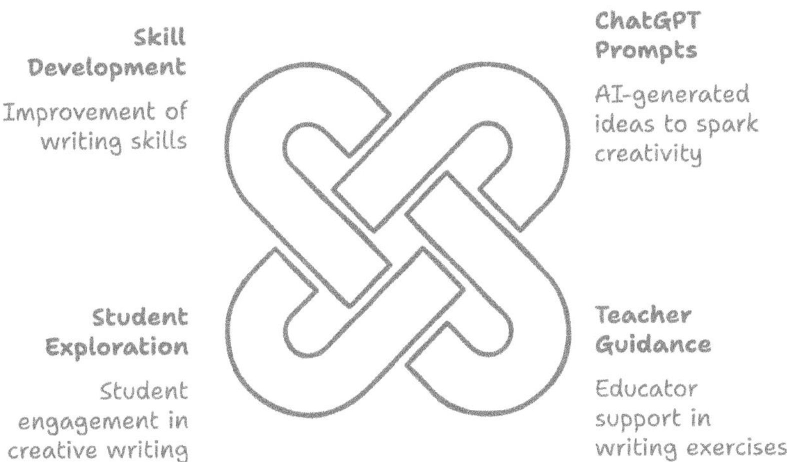

151. I need to know how to manage transitions between different activities smoothly.

152. Make suggestions about how to build routines in the classroom.

153. *Make suggestions for the establishment of a system that will reward appropriate behaviour.*

154. *In what manner should I treat pupils who persistently speak before their turn?*

155. *Make some suggestions for efficient methods of managing work done in groups.*

156. *Give some advice on dealing with pupils who refuse to participate in the activity.*

157. *How can I make a seating chart that reduces the number of distractions present?*

158. *Please provide suggestions on how to manage a large class efficiently.*

159. To calm down an overly exuberant class, please provide some ideas.

160. What is the best way for me to deal with kids who are chronically tardy to class?

161. Suggest ways to control the amount of noise in the classroom.

162. Please advise how to handle students who argue with their classmates.

163. How can I motivate kids to cooperate with the rules of the classroom?

164. Discuss potential solutions for dealing with pupils that are easily distracted.

165. *Ideas for managing a classroom with students of varying abilities should be provided.*

166. *What should I do if I encounter pupils who are disrespectful to their teachers?*

167. *Make suggestions for methods that can be used to manage excessively competitive pupils.*

168. *Offer advice on how to deal with kids who are continually distracted from their work.*

169. *What are some ways that I can make my classroom a more respectful place for my students?*

170. *Please suggest how to manage pupils who are excessively dependent on the instructor.*

171. Describe some strategies that can be used to deal with students who are always looking for attention.

172. Make some suggestions for how to deal with pupils who are experiencing excessive anxiety.

173. Make some suggestions for dealing with persistently disruptive students available.

174. How can I create an atmosphere in the classroom that encourages students to work together?

175. Provide suggestions for how to deal with very competitive students.

176. Offer suggestions for dealing with kids who are perpetually distracted from their work.

177. *What are some ways that I can make my classroom a more respectful place for my students?*

178. *Please suggest how to manage pupils who are excessively dependent on the instructor.*

179. *Describe some strategies that can be used to deal with students who are always looking for attention.*

180. *I am having trouble dealing with pupils that are resistant to receiving comments.*

181. *Make some suggestions for how to deal with pupils who are experiencing excessive anxiety.*

182. *Make some suggestions for dealing with persistently disruptive students available.*

183. *How can I create an atmosphere in the classroom that encourages students to work together?*

184. *Provide suggestions for how to deal with very competitive students.*

185. *Offer suggestions for dealing with kids who are perpetually distracted from their work.*

186. *What are some ways that I can make my classroom a more respectful place for my students?*

187. *Please suggest how to manage pupils who are excessively dependent on the instructor.*

188. *Describe some strategies that can be used to deal with students who are always looking for attention.*

189. *I am having trouble dealing with pupils that are resistant to receiving comments.*

190. *Make some suggestions for how to deal with pupils who are experiencing excessive anxiety.*

191. *Make some suggestions for dealing with persistently disruptive students available.*

192. *How can I create an atmosphere in the classroom that encourages students to work together?*

193. *Provide suggestions for how to deal with very competitive students.*

194. *Offer suggestions for dealing with kids who are perpetually distracted from their work.*

195. What are some ways that I can make my classroom a more respectful place for my students?

196. Please suggest how to manage pupils who are excessively dependent on the instructor.

197. Describe some strategies that can be used to deal with students who are always looking for attention.

198. Give students some innovative ideas for how they can be introduced to a new subject.

199. Think of ways to teach mathematical topics through the use of interactive games.

200. How can I encourage kids to take an interest in the history topics I teach?

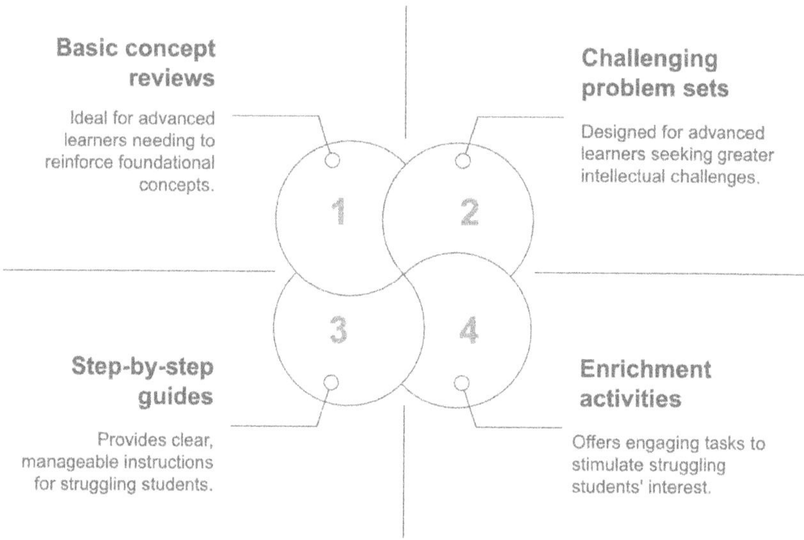

201. Discuss the various ways in which technology can be included in science classes.

202. To teach geography, please provide some ideas for hands-on activities.

203. When it comes to teaching literature, how can I employ storytelling?

204. Describe some ways in which grammar classes could be made more engaging.

205. To teach social studies, please provide some suggestions for incorporating role-playing.

206. What are some concrete examples that I can use to teach economics?

207. Provide suggestions for ways to make art classes more interesting.

208. Give some suggestions for how music might be used to teach poetry.

209. How can I use debates to teach skills related to critical thinking?

210. *Give some suggestions on how to make scientific experiments more interesting.*

211. *To educate problem-solving, please provide some suggestions for employing puzzles.*

212. *In what ways may I teach teamwork through the use of group projects?*

213. *To make maths teaching more relatable, please suggest some techniques.*

214. *Give some suggestions for how videos might be used to teach history.*

215. *How can I improve my vocabulary through the usage of games?*

216. *To make writing assignments more enjoyable, please suggest ideas.*

217. *To educate scientific concepts, please provide some suggestions for employing simulations.*

218. *When it comes to teaching about cultural diversity, how can I use storytelling?*

219. *You should suggest strategies to make the lessons in physical education more enjoyable.*

220. *To teach foreign languages, please provide some suggestions for employing technology.*

221. *How can I incorporate art projects into my lessons on history?*

222. *Suggest how to make the lessons on social studies more interactive.*

223. *To teach chemistry, please provide some suggestions for employing experiments.*

224. *When it comes to teaching literature, how can I use role-playing?*

225. *Give some suggestions on how to make maths classes more interactive.*

226. *Give some suggestions on how games might be used to educate geography.*

227. *In what ways may I use storytelling to teach concepts related to science?*

228. *Describe some ways in which history teachings can be made more approachable.*

• 43 •

229. *Make suggestions on how technology can be used to teach mathematics.*

230. *In the context of social studies, how can I make use of debates?*

231. *To make writing assignments more innovative, please suggest some techniques.*

232. *To teach history, please provide some suggestions for employing simulations.*

233. *Is it possible to teach economics through the use of role-playing?*

*234. Please suggest methods to make science classes more
interesting to students.*

• 44 •

*235. Give some examples of how puzzles can be used to teach
mathematics.*

*236. When it comes to teaching literature, how can I employ
storytelling?*

*237. Please suggest ways in which art classes could be made
more engaging.*

*238. Give some suggestions on how music might be used to
teach history.*

*239. How can I explain scientific principles through the use
of games?*

240. *Suggest how to make social studies courses more accessible.*

241. *To teach physics, please provide some suggestions for employing experiments.*

242. *When it comes to teaching geography, how can I employ role-playing?*

243. *Give some suggestions on how to make maths classes more interesting.*

244. *To teach literature, please provide some suggestions for using technology.*

245. *In what ways may I utilise discussions to teach topics related to science?*

246. *To make writing assignments more engaging, please suggest some ways.*

247. *To teach economics, please provide some suggestions for using simulations.*

248. *Make a test on the water cycle that consists of ten questions with multiple choice answers.*

249. *To teach fractions, please provide formative assessment options.*

250. *Describe some examples of constructive criticism that can be applied to student essays.*

Cycle of Personalized Feedback

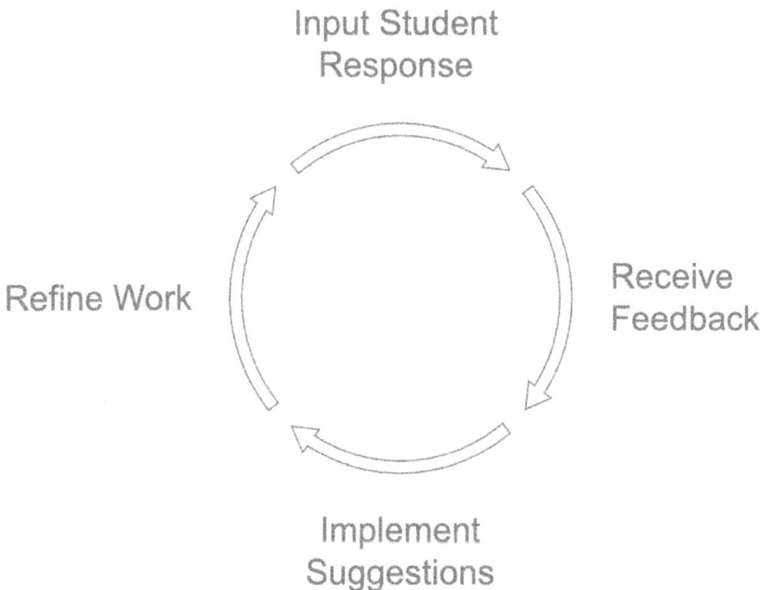

251. *Construct a checklist for students to use in their self-evaluation about the scientific process.*

252. *In the context of a history lesson, what are some good ways to employ peer assessment?*

253. *Make suggestions for how students' comprehension of a
book might be evaluated.*

254. *It would be helpful if you could provide some
suggestions for exit ticket questions for a maths session.*

255. *Develop a grading criteria for the presentations that
groups give on climate change.*

256. *How can I monitor my students' success in a scientific
class?*

257. *To urge pupils to write, you should suggest different
approaches to provide feedback.*

258. *Make a test on the American Revolution that consists of
ten questions that are either true or false.*

259. For teaching grammar, please provide formative assessment options.

260. Describe some examples of constructive criticism that can be applied to student efforts.

261. Students should receive a self-assessment checklist to evaluate their writing process.

262. In the context of a scientific class, what are some good ways to employ peer assessment?

263. Suqqest how students' comprehension of a historical event can be evaluated.

264. In the context of a literature class, please provide some suggestions for exit ticket questions.

265. The group presentations on ecosystems should be graded using a rubric you create.

266. How can I monitor my students' success in a maths class?

267. Suggest ways to deliver feedback to students in science that will motivate them.

268. Make a test about the solar system that consists of ten questions with multiple choice answers.

269. When it comes to teaching vocabulary, please provide some formative assessment procedures.

270. Give some examples of how students can receive constructive criticism for their presentations.

271. Construct a checklist for students to use in their self-evaluation about the scientific process.

272. What are some good ways to employ the peer assessment method in a math lesson?

273. Make suggestions for how students' comprehension of a poem can be evaluated.

274. Suggest questions that could be included on the exit ticket for a history class.

275. How can I monitor my students' success in a literature class?

276. Deliver suggestions for ways to deliver feedback to students in history that will motivate them.

277. *Make a test on the water cycle that consists of ten questions with true or false answers.*

278. *To teach fractions, please provide formative assessment options.*

279. *Describe some examples of constructive criticism that can be applied to student essays.*

280. *Construct a checklist for students to use in their self-evaluation about the scientific process.*

281. *In the context of a history lesson, what are some good ways to employ peer assessment?*

282. *Make suggestions for how students' comprehension of a book might be evaluated.*

283. It would be helpful if you could provide some suggestions for exit ticket questions for a maths session.

284. Develop a grading criteria for the presentations that groups give on climate change.

285. How can I monitor my students' success in a scientific class?

286. To urge pupils to write, you should suggest different approaches to provide feedback.

287. For teaching grammar, please provide formative assessment options.

288. Describe some examples of constructive criticism that can be applied to student efforts.

289. *Students should receive a self-assessment checklist to evaluate their writing process.*

290. *In the context of a scientific class, what are some good ways to employ peer assessment?*

291. *Suggest how students' comprehension of a historical event can be evaluated.*

292. *In the context of a literature class, please provide some suggestions for exit ticket questions.*

293. *The group presentations on ecosystems should be graded using a rubric you create.*

294. *How can I monitor my students' success in a maths class?*

295. *Suggest ways to deliver feedback to students in science that will motivate them.*

296. *Suggest educational apps that can be used to educate elementary school pupils in mathematics.*

297. *What efficient ways to use Google Classroom to stay on top of my assignments?*

298. *Ideas for using virtual reality in historical education should be provided.*

299. *Please suggest several ways that students in middle school can learn to code.*

300. *How do I make science-related video tutorials that are interesting to watch?*

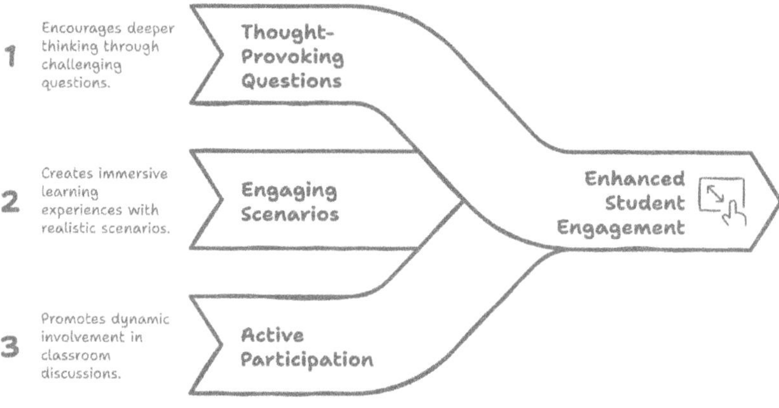

301. Educate students on how to make effective use of interactive whiteboards in the classroom.

302. Explain how artificial intelligence techniques could be included in language arts classes.

303. How can I use social media to improve the learning experience for my students?

304. In social studies, please provide suggestions for online collaborative projects.

305. Please provide suggestions on how students in high school might learn about digital citizenship.

306. How do I make use of Kahoot! to go over the content before taking a test?

307. Give some suggestions on how students might use Flipgrid to increase their level of participation.

308. Give some suggestions on how Padlet might be used for brainstorming sessions.

309. What are some successful ways I can incorporate YouTube films into my lessons?

310. *Give some advice on using Zoom for virtual conferences between teachers and parents.*

311. *Please provide suggestions on how to use Canva to create resources for the classroom.*

312. *What is the best way to use Quizlet to assist kids in their vocabulary study?*

313. *What are some ways that you may use Nearpod to make your lessons more interactive?*

314. *What is the best way to use Google Forms to generate self-grading quizzes?*

315. *Make suggestions for how Scratch might be used to teach fundamentals of coding.*

316. *Regarding geography classes, please suggest ways to use Google Earth.*

317. *You should provide some pointers on how to use Zoom breakout rooms for collaborative work.*

318. *Give some suggestions on how students might use Google Slides for their presentations.*

319. *What is the best way to utilise Flipgrid to get feedback from my peers on tasks?*

320. *Make suggestions for how Microsoft Teams might be used to facilitate collaboration in the classroom.*

321. *Give some suggestions on how Tinkercad might be used for 3D design projects.*

322. Please provide some pointers on how to use Screencastify to generate instructional movies.

323. Suggest different methods that students can utilise Book Creator to share their stories.

324. What is the best way to organise my lesson plans using Google Keep?

325. Give some suggestions on how Wakelet might be used to curate educational content.

326. In the context of multimedia projects, please suggest ways to use Adobe Spark.

327. How can I use Google Drawings to create diagrams that involve multiple people?

328. *If you want to check for understanding, suggest how to use Zoom polls.*

329. *In the context of student portfolios, please suggest ways to leverage Google Sites.*

330. *When it comes to scheduling activities for the classroom, how can I use Google Calendar?*

331. *Give students some suggestions on how they might use WeVideo for their video projects.*

332. *How can I use Google Sheets to monitor my students' progress?*

333. *What are some helpful hints for conducting student surveys using Google Forms?*

*334. Please provide suggestions on how Google Classroom
can be used for flipped learning.*

*335. What is the best way to host virtual guest speakers
using Google Meet?*

*336. Please suggest how Google Arts & Culture might be
utilised in art classes.*

*337. Please suggest how Google Translate can benefit
students learning English as a second language.*

*338. Can you tell me how to use Google Scholar for my
research work as a student?*

*339. Please recommend books that will help improve your
ability to manage a classroom.*

340. Offer advice on how to successfully juggle the demands of teaching with those of your personal life.

341. How can I always be current on the most recent educational trends?

342. Please suggest methods in which you and your colleagues might work together to plan lessons.

343. Offer suggestions for presentations that can be given at educational conferences.

344. With reflective journaling, how can I make my teaching more effective?

345. For professional growth in STEM fields, suggest online courses.

346. The provision of appropriate mentoring programs for new teachers is crucial.

347. What are some ways that I might introduce mindfulness into my daily routine?

348. Please provide various methods to construct a professional learning network (PLN).

349. What are some ways that I can use social media to advance my career?

350. Give some suggestions for attending conferences that are held online for education.

Educational Content Generation Process

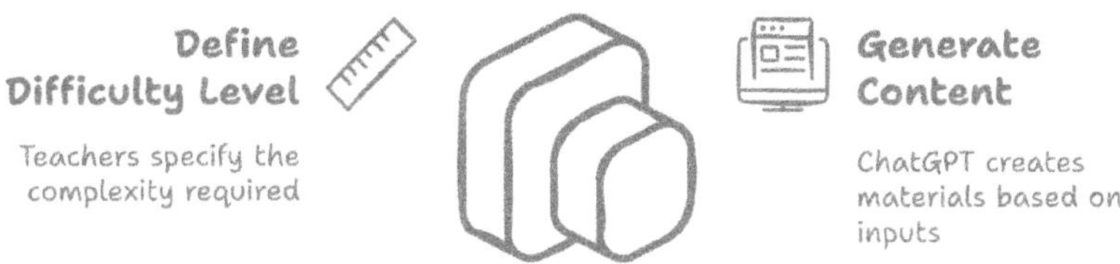

351. *Give some suggestions on how to maintain motivation when things are difficult.*

352. *How can I increase my professional skills through the usage of podcasts?*

353. *Please provide some advice on how to create a plan for professional development.*

354. *If you are a teacher, please suggest ideas to enhance your time management.*

355. *What are some ways that I can use webinars to discover new methods of instruction?*

356. *Describe some potential ways in which instructors from different schools could work together.*

357. *Make suggestions on methods to increase observational abilities in the classroom.*

358. *How can I make use of action research to enhance my teaching pedagogy?*

359. *We want to offer some advice on how to write papers for educational magazines.*

360. *Please suggest ideas to improve the skills of providing comments on student work.*

361. How can I use the observations of my peers to improve
my teaching skills?

362. To create a teaching portfolio, please provide some
suggestions.

363. Share your ideas on how to enhance communication
skills between teachers and parents.

364. What are some ways that I can use data to inform my
teaching approach?

365. During the academic year, please provide some advice
on how to deal with stress.

366. Please suggest methods to increase the effectiveness of
lesson planning.

*367. For the sake of professional development, how can I
make use of online forums?*

•

*368. What ideas can be used to develop a personal teaching
philosophy?*

*369. Suggest methods to increase students' ability to use
technology in the classroom.*

*370. What is the best way for me to communicate with other
educators through Twitter?*

*371. Please provide some pointers on how to write
instructional objectives effectively.*

*372. Provide suggestions on methods to develop abilities in
assessment design.*

373. *Can you tell me how to use LinkedIn to network with other professionals?*

374. *Ideas for the creation of a blog for professional growth should be provided.*

375. *Kindly suggest ways in which differentiation techniques can be improved.*

376. *What are some ways that I can use YouTube to advance my career?*

377. *Please provide some pointers on how to write student recommendations effectively.*

378. *Make suggestions on methods to improve the ability to organise the classroom.*

379. What is the best way to use Pinterest to get ideas for my classroom?

380. Offer suggestions for the production of a podcast devoted to professional growth.

381. Provide suggestions on how to strengthen initiatives for student involvement.

382. What is the best way to use Instagram to showcase activities from the classroom?

383. Please provide some advice on how to write grant applications effectively.

384. Make some suggestions on how to improve the methods of classroom management.

385. *For the sake of professional development, how can I make use of Facebook groups?*

386. *Please provide suggestions for the creation of a video series for professional development.*

387. *Create an email that extends a warm greeting to parents at the beginning of the school year.*

388. *Describe some strategies that can be used to make parent-teacher conferences more productive.*

389. *Suggest how parents might be informed about their children's progress.*

390. *What are some ways that I can interact with parents in the classroom?*

391. *Create a message to send to parents informing them of an impending excursion.*

392. *Please suggest how to get parents involved in their children's homework.*

293. *What are some ways that I can communicate with my parents using technology?*

294. *Please provide suggestions for evenings of family engagement.*

395. *Please provide suggestions on how to manage challenging conversations with parents.*

396. *Create a newsletter for parents that contains information on the latest classroom developments.*

397. Please provide some advice on how to create a conversation log for parents.

398. Put up ideas on how parents might recognise the accomplishments of their children.

399. What is the best way for me to communicate with parents using ClassDojo?

400. Give some suggestions for holding meetings between teachers and parents online.

Unleashing ChatGPT's Potential in Education

401. Please suggest methods in which parents might participate in school events.

402. What are some ways that I can utilise email to communicate positive feedback to parents?

403. To create a parent volunteer program, please provide some tips.

404. Offer suggestions on how to discuss academic issues with parents.

405. What are some ways that I can engage parents when using social media?

406. Draft a letter to parents informing them of the expectations for the classroom.

407. *To establish trust with parents, you should provide strategies.*

408. *Please suggest ways in which parents might participate in student projects.*

409. *What is the best way to obtain input from parents using Google Forms?*

410. *Offer suggestions for the establishment of a resource centre for parents.*

411. *Provide suggestions for teaching parents about the rules of the classroom.*

412. *How can I use Remind to e-mail parents with the latest information?*

413. I want to offer some advice on managing behavioural concerns with parents.

414. Please suggest ways parents can be involved in the decision-making process at the school.

415. What is the best way to interact with my parents using video messages?

416. Compose a letter to parents regarding the policies around homework.

417. Offer solutions to the problems that parents face with their children's attendance.

418. Make suggestions for methods in which parents might participate in extracurricular activities.

419. *What is best for me to interact with parents through a class website?*

420. *Suggest forming a parent-teacher organisation (known as a PTA).*

421. *Provide suggestions for parents on how to address issues with technology.*

422. *What is the best way to use newsletters to convey highlights from the classroom?*

423. *Share some advice with parents on how to meet their children's special education requirements.*

424. *Ideas for getting parents involved in school fundraising should be provided.*

425. In what ways can I utilise surveys to collect feedback from parents?

426. When it comes to standardised testing, you should write a letter to parents.

427. It is essential to provide parents with strategies for handling issues around bullying.

428. Make suggestions for methods in which parents might participate in school safety activities.

429. What are the best ways to use email to share classroom resources with parents?

430. Please provide some thoughts on creating a parent guide.

431. Provide suggestions for how to approach concerns around mental health with parents.

432. How may I utilise social media to communicate updates about my classroom?

433. Advise how to deal with the pressure from academics with parents.

434. What are some ways parents can be involved in planning school improvement?

435. Provide some suggestions for teaching students who have attention-deficit/hyperactivity disorder (ADHD).

436. I have kids who have dyslexia; how can I modify the lessons for them?

437. Kindly provide ways in which an inclusive classroom
climate can be created.

438. Help students with autism by providing them with
educational resources.

439. In what ways may I make use of assistive technology in
the classroom?

440. Offer suggestions for differentiating the teaching
approach for gifted pupils.

441. Where can I find support for pupils struggling with
emotional and behavioural issues?

442. Make suggestions for methods to work together with the
staff of special education.

443. Help pupils who have hearing issues by providing them with suggestions for teaching.

444. Please suggest several ways to modify evaluations for students with individualised education programs (IEPs).

445. What are some ways that I can make my classroom more sensory-friendly?

446. What are some helpful hints for instructing pupils who have physical disabilities?

447. Make suggestions for methods in which parents of students with special needs might be involved.

448. How can I implement Universal Design for Learning (UDL) in my classroom?

449. Give some suggestions for teaching pupils who are experiencing speech delays.

• 82 •

450. Suggest how the needs of twice outstanding students can be met.

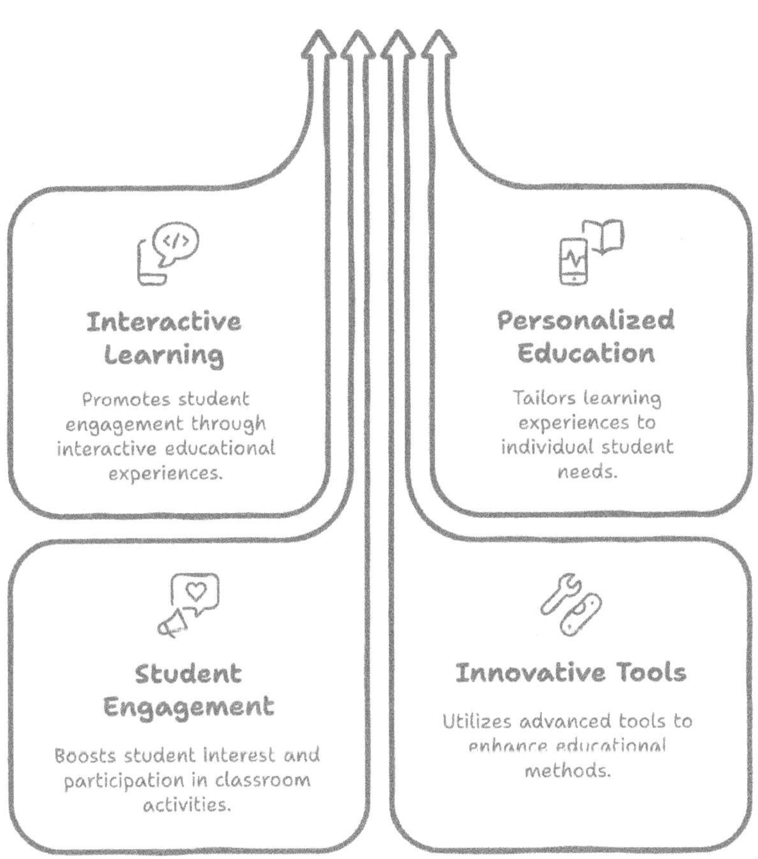

451. How can I use peer tutoring to support children with special needs?

452. *Make some suggestions for the development of individualised learning plans.*

453. *What are some ways that I can use visual aids to assist students who have special needs?*

454. *Consider the following suggestions for instructing students who have intellectual challenges.*

455. *Provide suggestions on how pupils' social and emotional needs might be addressed.*

456. *For pupils who have special needs, what are some ways that I might employ positive reinforcement?*

457. *Give some advice on how to instruct kids who have had traumatic brain injuries.*

458. *Make some suggestions for how the needs of kids who suffer from anxiety disorders can be met.*

459. *What are some ways that I might accommodate students who have special needs by using flexible seating?*

460. *For students who have Down syndrome, please provide some ideas for teaching.*

461. *Make some suggestions for how the needs of students who have ADHD can be met.*

462. *What are some ways that I might encourage children who have special needs to use fidget tools?*

463. *Make some suggestions for how the needs of pupils who have autism can be met.*

464. *Using social tales to support kids with special needs: how can I do this?*

465. *Ideas for teaching students who are experiencing emotional disturbances should be provided.*

466. *Suggest how the needs of pupils with dyslexia can be addressed.*

467. *Using graphic organisers to serve students who have unique needs: what are some ways I can do this?*

468. *Please provide suggestions about how the needs of kids with visual impairments can be met.*

469. *In what ways can I make use of technology to assist kids who have specific difficulties?*

470. *Consider the following suggestions for instructing students who have physical limitations.*

471. *Give some suggestions on how to meet the requirements of pupils who have speech delays.*

472. *How can I use peer mentoring to assist students with special needs?*

473. *Make some suggestions for the development of individualised learning plans.*

474. *What are some ways that I can use visual aids to assist students who have special needs?*

475. *Consider the following suggestions for instructing students who have intellectual challenges.*

476. *Provide suggestions on how pupils' social and emotional needs might be addressed.*

477. *For pupils who have special needs, what are some ways that I might employ positive reinforcement?*

478. *Give some advice on how to instruct kids who have had traumatic brain injuries.*

479. *You should suggest art projects relevant to the solar system for primary school pupils.*

480. *Give some suggestions for scientific experiments that can be done with ordinary household objects.*

481. *To teach about historical events, you should provide some suggestions for theatre exercises.*

482. *For a classroom quiz game, you should suggest some fun trivia questions.*

483. *Please provide suggestions for activities that might be used in the classroom to celebrate cultural diversity.*

484. *Give some suggestions on how music could be used in a history lesson.*

485. *To celebrate the conclusion of the school year, please provide some suggestions.*

486. *Scavenger hunts are an excellent method to educate*

geography, so offer some suggestions.

487. *Describe some activities that can be used to teach fractions through cooking.*

488. *In the context of art projects, please suggest approaches to teach poetry.*

489. *Make suggestions on how science might be taught through nature walks.*

490. *Ideas for teaching history through the use of role-playing games are welcome.*

491. *Offer suggestions on using board games as a means of teaching mathematics.*

492. *Please suggest several ways that creative storytelling can be used to teach literature.*

493. *Please provide suggestions for using simulated elections as a teaching tool for social studies.*

494. *Explore the use of do-it-yourself experiments as a means of teaching science.*

495. *Assist with developing fun games that can be used to teach grammar.*

496. *In the context of teaching vocabulary, please suggest ways to use crossword puzzles.*

497. *You should provide some suggestions for teaching geography through activities that involve making maps.*

498. *Give some suggestions for teaching mathematics through the use of sports statistics.*

499. Help me think of ways to teach science through activities that involve gardening.

500. Offer suggestions for the teaching of literature through the use of book clubs.

Integrating ChatGPT in Education

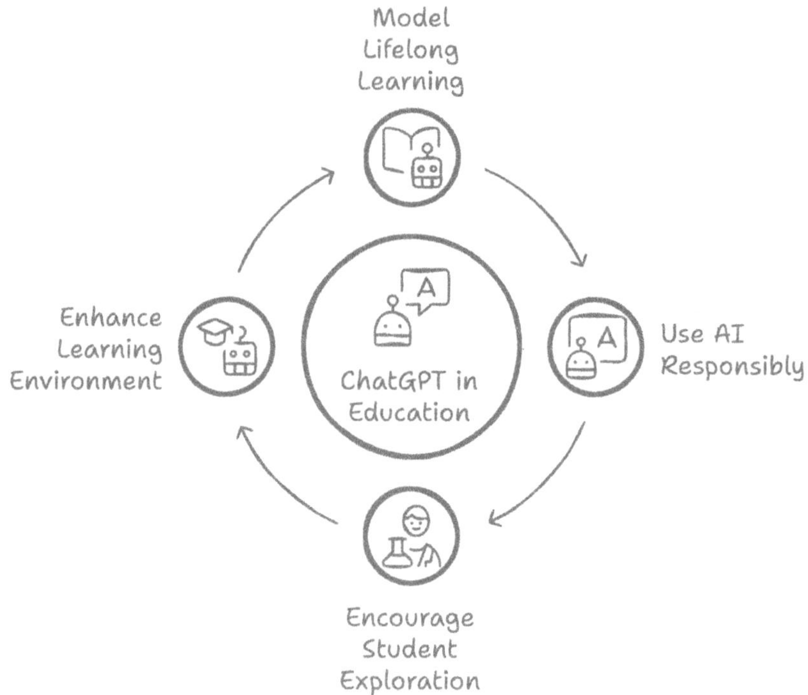

II

Podcast: Using ChatGPT!

Get the Best of Learning ChatGPT!

III

Video Based Learning: Using ChatGPT!

Great! Here's a helpful video to learn ChatGPT step-by-step:

Dr Dheeraj Mehrotra, Regional Head of Adani GEMS Education in India, is a distinguished educational leader and innovator with over three decades of experience transforming education through excellence and innovation. A recipient of the President of India's National Teacher Award (2006), he is a certified expert in Six Sigma (White and Yellow Belt), Neuro-Linguistic Programming (NLP), and Total Quality Management (TQM). His specialisation encompasses academic audits, school quality assurance and accreditation (SQAA), and implementing Kaizen and 5S in schools. As an accomplished author, Dr Mehrotra has published over 200 books on various subjects, including computer science, artificial intelligence, digital body language, quality circles, and school management. His contributions also include the development of more than 150 free educational mobile apps for teachers, students, and parents, a feat recognised by the Limca Book of Records and the India Book of Records. Dr Mehrotra has served as Principal at prestigious institutions such as De Indian Public School in New Delhi, NPS International School in Guwahati, and Kunwar's Global School in Lucknow. He has also held the position of Education Officer at GEMS in Gurgaon, making significant contributions to the global education community. As a premier UDEMY instructor, Dr Mehrotra has created over 500 courses that have impacted more than 800,000 learners across 180 countries. Additionally, as the founder and president of the IoT Society of India, he advocates for the integration of technology in education worldwide.

Scan Here
FOR QUALITY BOOKS
For Home Library for
Parents, Educators & Students

BOOKS BY THE SAME AUTHOR